TRAGIC EVENT RESPONSE TEAM

SUPPORT SERVICES

I FEEL SAD

A RESOURCE ON LOSS AND GRIEF FOR PRIMARY/JUNIOR TEACHERS

Louis

I Feel Sad

A Resource on Loss and Grief for Primary/Junior Teachers

Cathy Gross

Sharron McKeever

Mary Ann Takacs Debly

NOVALIS

© 2007 Novalis, Saint Paul University, Ottawa, Canada

Cover design and layout: Audrey Wells

Business Offices:
Novalis Publishing Inc.
10 Lower Spadina Avenue, Suite 400
Toronto, Ontario, Canada
M5V 2Z2

Novalis Publishing Inc.
4475 Frontenac Street
Montréal, Québec, Canada
H2H 2S2

Phone: 1-800-387-7164
Fax: 1-800-204-4140
E-mail: books@novalis.ca
www.novalis.ca

Library and Archives Canada Cataloguing in Publication

Gross, Cathy
    I feel sad : a resource on loss and grief for primary/junior teachers / Cathy Gross, Shar-
ron McKeever, Mary Ann Takacs Debly.

Includes bibliographical references.
ISBN-13: 978-2-89507-830-2
ISBN-10: 2-89507-830-0

    1. Grief in children. 2. Loss (Psychology) in children. I. McKeever, Sharron, II. Takacs
Debly, Mary Ann III. Title.

BF723.L68G76 2006   155.9'3   C2006-905807-5

Printed in Canada.

We acknowledge the financial support of the Government of Canada through the Book Publishing Industry Development Program (BPIDP) for our publishing activities.

5   4   3   2   1   11   10   09   08   07

CONTENTS

Preface

Dear Teacher,

As educators, regardless of the role we play in the school community, we have the privileged vocation of helping to form our students. We journey with them through sunny days of joyful successes and stormy days of challenging difficulties. Some of our students struggle with losses in their lives. How can we support them during these painful times?

As teachers and Religion and Family Life Education consultants with 102 years of combined experience, we have had the honour of walking with and supporting students and staff as they wrestled with a wide range of life's losses. This resource is the fruit of our experiences and of the wisdom we gained over the years. We are pleased to share it with you.

Our hope is that the ideas we offer here will give you confidence and a sense of direction when you are called to support individuals, a class or the entire school community in times of loss or crisis. Perhaps the ideas in this resource will invite conversation and discussion in the staff room as well. You can't plan ahead for difficult events in the lives of your students or your school, but you can develop some insights and wisdom that will anchor you when dealing with loss.

All of us who lovingly embrace this ministry of accompanying others through loss are so blessed to have Jesus as our foundation – our guide. Jesus tells us, "I am the way, and the truth, and the life" (John 14:6). Jesus will never leave us; he stays with us in joy and in sorrow. As he reminds his disciples, "Remember, I am with you always, to the end of the age" (Matthew 28:20).

With our best wishes,

Cathy, Sharron and Mary Ann

I

An Introduction to Loss and Grief

This resource gives you the tools you need to support your students when they experience loss in their lives. It has been created to guide you as you assist students who are journeying through the grieving process, offer them hope, and eventually help them accept their loss with courage.

As much as you might want to, you cannot eliminate all pain and suffering from the lives of your students. By acknowledging Christ's presence even in the sadness and pain of loss, you provide students with meaning and hope. You do this by placing faith at the heart of the grieving process and by recognizing that Jesus always walks with us, even in life's darkest moments.

What is loss?

A loss is any personal sense of being deprived of something important. Feelings of loss are common to all of us, and each loss, whether it seems trivial or serious to us or to other people, has the potential to shape who we are and how we perceive ourselves in relationship to others. Our losses can have a profound effect that will extend across the whole of our lives.

Children may experience some of the following losses.

Obvious Sources of Loss

- death of someone important (including miscarriage);

- loss of a pet (a pet that has died, run away or had to be given away for some reason);

- moving (or a close friend moving);

- changing schools;

- divorce;

- loss of friendship;

- not fitting in;

- not being chosen for a team or group;

- a parent's loss of employment;

- loss of home;

- theft;

- family events (chronic illness, grandparent moving in, new baby);

- an older sibling leaving for college, university or work.

Less Obvious Sources of Loss

- hospitalization;

- long periods of separation from a parent;

- bullying;

- being the subject of lies or gossip;

- abuse (sexual, physical, emotional);

- alcoholism in the family;

- humiliation (especially in front of peers);

- change of country or nationality;

- natural disasters;

- repeated failure;

- shattered fantasies (Santa Claus, Tooth Fairy, Easter Bunny, fallen heroes).

What is grief?

Grief is the name given to the myriad emotions we feel in response to loss. Grieving is a complex process of gradually integrating the loss we have endured and, ultimately, once again finding meaning and purpose in life. There is no one way to describe grief.

People experience a broad range of feelings after a loss. Some feel anger, guilt and alienation, while others feel hopelessness and despair. Not everyone will have the same quantity or intensity of feelings. Children in the same family may exhibit different emotions and respond in different ways to the same loss.

As a teacher, allow your students to grieve in whatever way is best for them. At the same time, be aware that some kinds of behaviour can be harmful to the students themselves or to others. If you see this kind of behaviour, offer more intervention or seek professional help for the student (see Chapter 3).

The grieving process

Grieving is hard work. When life has been altered irrevocably, sometimes it is all a person can do just to get out of bed in the morning and face a new day. Whatever the source of the loss – a divorce, a move, the loss of a friendship, or the death of a loved one (including that of a pet) – grieving involves a journey. No matter what age the grief-stricken person is, there are three main stages in grieving:

- confusion and shock;

- helplessness and despair; and

- acceptance and integration of the loss into life.

Emotional responses to loss do not necessarily follow this order. Very often a person will move back and forth from acceptance to confusion and despair. No one "gets over" a significant loss – but people can and do learn to live with their loss.

A major life loss, such as divorce, can take anywhere from a few years to a lifetime to become fully integrated in a person's life. In the grieving process, the immediate intense emotions eventually subside. It might seem that the worst pain is over. Then something can occur that triggers the intense feelings again. For example, a person who has gone through a divorce may find painful feelings resurfacing when supporting a close friend struggling with a marriage breakup. Over time, the intensity and frequency of these feelings do lessen. But they are never completely gone.

Throughout life, a single loss can continue to call up feelings of grief – not just for the loss itself, but also for the loss of all that might have been. For example, the loss of a parent is grieved immediately, because the person is gone from our presence at this moment in our life. As the years pass, precious moments that might have been shared with that parent are also experienced as loss, and grief is revisited. For young adults, these precious moments might include graduation, a first job, marriage or the birth of a child. They realize as these events occur that they have no father to share their successes, no grandfather to hug their grandchildren and sing them to sleep.

The aim of the grieving process is to allow people to move through the experience of loss and re-establish emotional energy into their lives. Healthy grieving results in a forward movement and making new connections in life. For example, after the loss of a friend, the process of grieving helps a person accept the finality of that loss and then move forward to build new friendships. If the grieving process cannot be completed in a healthy way, however, the grieving person may become withdrawn, afraid to make new friends for fear of further loss, and be unable to re-engage with life.

A healthy grieving process contains several essential components.

1. Accepting that the loss is real

When a loved one dies, we must accept that they cannot come back. After a divorce, family members need to acknowledge that they will not live together again. When a friend moves to another country, we must face the fact that we may fall out of touch. In each situation, as we grieve we must realize and accept that what we have lost cannot be retrieved; the separation is final. There is a division between life before the loss and the new reality that follows. Integrating this new reality takes time and is very painful, but it is essential for healthy grieving.

2. Experiencing the pain of the loss

The overwhelming pain and other feelings linked to loss are indispensable steps on the road to healing. Stuffing the feelings inside, running away from them or following other people's ideas of how we "should" feel only hinders the healing. Fortunate are we if we have someone who will listen to our story without judging, and who is strong enough to let us cry.

3. Adjusting to the changed environment

After a loss, life is now different. As we become aware of the changes in our lives, we may need to learn some new skills, such as finding fresh ways of doing things or relating to others. That growing awareness means we are beginning to be at home within the changed context of our life.

4. *Reinvesting emotional energy into other relationships or activities*

This difficult task requires that we integrate the experience of loss into our past understanding of life so that we can place our emotional energy into a new beginning. This turn to the future might feel like a betrayal, but accepting the loss does not mean we don't care. Rather, it means that we are ready to carry on, enriched by memories of persons, things and events that have formed us in the past and will continue to be a part of our lives in the future.

5. *Reconciling and forgiving*

If anger is involved in the loss, forgiveness and reconciliation may be necessary components of the grieving process. When moving forward after a divorce, for example, spouses may be angry at each other, or the children may be angry with one or both parents. When someone dies, we may be angry with that person for leaving us alone. Family members may be angry with a parent who accepts a job that requires all of them to move, disrupting friendships, school life and much more. Forgiveness and reconciliation can be a key part of a healthy grieving process. Even if we can never rekindle the relationship, letting go of bitterness, anger or the desire for revenge frees us to move on with our lives.

God is with us in our grief

When students question the actions or presence of God in their loss, it is important to communicate to them that loss is truly a mystery. God does not plan or desire their loss. God does not cause death or natural disasters. As Christians, the most important truth we can hold on to is that we know truly and unshakably that God is always with us. God loves us deeply and is present with us in our loss and in all the suffering it brings.

Turning to God at times of loss is very important, but at first, offering your thoughts about God may short-circuit a student's ability to begin grieving. People who are grieving must begin by getting in touch with their authentic feelings. A more appropriate time to begin discussing the presence of God as a source of peace, hope and new directions is after authentic feelings have been acknowledged and expressed.

As difficult as it may seem at the time of a painful loss, new life can come from the experience if we are patient and willing to open ourselves to new possibilities. We need to trust that God is right there with us and will stay with us as we work through the pain of the loss.

Conclusion

The journey of the grieving process is open-ended. There are no set timelines for expressing feelings and no one way to express them. Each person's grief journey is unique, just as the gift of each life is a unique and precious part of God's creation.

2

How Children Grieve

As we saw in Chapter 1, children can experience a wide variety of losses. It might seem that the death of a goldfish would be less disruptive than a major move or the loss of a parent's job, but this is not necessarily the case. Perhaps, for your student, the death of the goldfish is a more concrete form of loss than the anxiety associated with a serious ongoing disruption in the family, such as an impending move, a job loss or a serious illness. Your students need permission to grieve, whatever the loss. Give them time, care and support to help them navigate a troubling period in their lives.

Aspects of the grieving process for children

Children have their own way of grieving. Here are three aspects of the grieving process that you might see in your young students.

1. *Grieving is sporadic*

Because they cannot sustain continual and intense emotional and behavioural grief, young children grieve in a way that tends to be sporadic rather than orderly and predictable. Adults are often surprised when children go from crying to playing and laughing, seemingly recovered from their sadness. This behaviour does not mean that their grieving is over. Their minds seem to protect them from what might be too powerful to handle all at once, but they will come back to their grief again in the future.

2. *Grieving lasts a long time*

Although children may outwardly show grief only occasionally and briefly (thus giving adults the false impression that they are handling things very well), in reality a child's grieving process usually lasts longer than an adult's. Grief is revisited again and again at different stages of development; special times such as graduation, marriage or a birth can cause feelings of grief to resurface. We all mourn both the initial separation of any loss and the lost potential of that separation throughout our lives. A 90-year-old woman can occasionally mourn the mother-daughter relationship she missed as a result of her mother's death more than 80 years earlier.

3. *Grieving is influenced by culture and social norms*

Although grief is a universal experience, crossing all ages and cultures, how people grieve and mourn reflects their religious, social and cultural background. Teachers in Catholic schools cannot assume a homogenous system of belief and practice among students. Not only are there a wide variety of Christian cultures and social practices within your classroom, you likely have students from interfaith families as well. Be sensitive to the religious, social and cultural background of a grieving student in your class.

Grief and child development

How children grieve is also influenced by their age and stage of development. The following profiles outline how a child's cognitive and emotional stage of development can affect his or her understanding and expression of loss.

Very young children (ages 3 to 5: Junior and Senior Kindergarten)

- *Concrete thinking* – Children of this age have so little sense of history that they cannot understand abstract concepts such as finality, permanence and irreversibility. They may, for example, expect a dead person to return. They might imagine that someone who has died can move, eat, see and hear. They need to be gently reminded that dead people or pets do not breathe or feel anything. They don't "live" in cemeteries and they cannot come back to life. Children who have recently moved will struggle to understand that they will not go back to their old house or country. If there has been a divorce in their family, they will have difficulty understanding that Mom and Dad will not live together again and that they will be a family in a new way.

- *Magical thinking* – Many young children believe that their thoughts can cause someone to get sick and die or move away.

- *Egocentricity* – Very young children understand the world only in terms of themselves. They are concerned with physical needs, and their concept of time is "now." Sometimes they will have an underlying fear about who will take care of them, and may regress to baby-like behaviour, such as bed-wetting or wanting to be carried.

- *Dramatizing feelings* – Young children may play out their feelings of grief through activities such as playing funeral, going to the hospital, or getting ready to move.

- *Physical symptoms* – Young children may experience their grief through physical symptoms, such as headaches, stomach aches, or having trouble eating or sleeping.

- *Emotional needs* – Young children need ongoing calm, soothing emotional support with appropriate physical contact. They need repeated reassurance that they are still loved and will be cared for.

- *Play patterns* – Because very young children have a short attention span and a limit to the amount of information they can retain, their grieving behaviour may surprise adults. They may need to ask the same question about the loss repeatedly, and may move from times of crying and being upset to "normal" play. (Playing does not indicate that they do not feel hurt and sad.)

Primary Students (ages 6 to 8: grades 1 to 3)

- *Fantasy thinking* – 6- to 8-year-old children enjoy stories of fantasy and monsters. For them, death is often a person out there who wants to catch them. They think they can avoid being caught by being good.

- *Concrete thinking* – Children of this age still think very concretely. You will need to repeat clear, factual information in a reassuring manner.

- *Fascination with fear* – Many children have an almost ghoulish fascination with skeletons, ghosts, witches, monsters, graveyards, haunted houses, "bad" people, darkness and being alone. They may also be fascinated with the details about decomposition.

- *Perceptions of death* – Children at this age perceive death as something that happens primarily to old people. They find the death of a young person or sibling very difficult to understand.

- *Range of behaviours* – Children respond to loss with a range of behaviours, which might include fear of school; learning problems; or aggressive, destructive or antisocial actions (often found in boys). They may withdraw from friends and activities or become overattached to adults.

- *Beginning awareness* – Some children will begin to distinguish between the imaginary world of cartoons and games and the finality of their real-life losses. There is a growing awareness of universality, causality, irreversibility.

- *Physical responses* – Children at this age may also exhibit physical responses to loss, such as fatigue, stomach aches, sore throats, headaches or insomnia.

Junior Division Students (ages 9 to 12: grades 4 to 6)

- *Cognitive development* – These children are capable of understanding the finality of their loss. They can grasp the concepts of permanence, irreversibility and causality.

- *Increased anxiety* – Because of their greater understanding of the reality of loss, they may have increased anxiety about how it will affect their lives. If their parents are fighting, they may fear a divorce is imminent. If a friend is excluded from their group, they may fear they will be next.

- *Emotional expression* – Because children do not have the language to express their feelings of loss, they may choose indirect methods, such as withdrawing from relationships, behaving aggressively, covering up their emotions and trying to appear normal by joking, acting tough or appearing cool or in control. Underneath this behaviour, they are deeply sad and frightened.

- *Physical symptoms* – Children of this age may have difficulty concentrating, have trouble with schoolwork, be persistently angry or sad, engage in impulsive behaviour, have physical complaints (with constant fatigue), or change their eating habits. Some children might start overachieving and put pressure on themselves with a need for perfection.

Unresolved Grief

If children are unable to grieve properly the losses they encounter in their early years, their unresolved grief will be a block in their development toward full maturity as adults. Unresolved grief can contribute to destructive escape mechanisms, such as addictive behaviour or the inability to form intimate relationships in later teen and adult years.

Conclusion

Although it is painful to see children hurting, honour their right and need to grieve. As their teacher, feel privileged to accompany your students through the grieving process – from the first protest and denial of their changed circumstance, through the pain, despair and disorganization of recognizing the finality of their loss, to their re-engagement with life. You have a special place in the lives of your students as they grieve – embrace it!

3

JOURNEYING WITH THE GRIEVING STUDENT

Your own grief history

One of the best ways to begin preparing yourself to help grieving students is to look at your own experiences of grief. Loss and grief in your own life can help you understand grieving students better, but at the same time can make it difficult for you to help them. For instance, if your marriage ended recently, it may be hard for you to encourage a student who is struggling with how to remain faithful to both divorcing parents.

A *personal story*

In 1995, I was teaching Grade 11 Religion. My father, who had Alzheimer's disease, was in a nursing home. Students were invited to begin each class with their own choice of prayer. One day, two young women began with Robert Munsch's children's book Love You Forever, *which tells the story of the never-ending love between parent and child. At first, my tears were gentle, but soon I was sobbing. The entire class – boys and girls – gathered around, caring for and comforting me. They were equally caring a few months later, when my father died. At the end of the year, they rejoiced with me when my second grandson was born.*

That same year, two of my students each lost a parent to death. Who ministered to whom? There was no formal program, but we all experienced care, concern and support even as everyday life in Grade 11 went on.

Cathy Gross   23

We share this story for two reasons. First, it is impossible to know when loss will meet you face to face, either personally or through your students. Second, it is important to have some awareness of loss and grief in your own life so you will not be overwhelmed as you walk with your grieving students. There are times when you may be in such a fragile state that you cannot help a student in pain. If someone close to you is dying or has recently died, your marriage has just broken up, or your last child has just left for university, you may need to pull back for a while and allow the strength of your colleagues to accompany that young person. Teamwork is more than just sharing ideas and lesson plans; recognizing your own need is strength, not weakness.

Talking with a friend, colleague, pastor or counsellor about unresolved or ongoing personal difficulties in your life would help. If this is not possible, the following questions might be a useful guide for generating a personal inventory of your own grief experiences. This list is not exhaustive; considering these experiences may prompt you to think of others.

A personal inventory of grief

- What is the first significant loss you can remember?

- How did you learn about that loss?

- Did you feel left out? Did your family try to protect you from the reality even though you knew something was wrong?

- What feelings did you have?

- Were there questions you wanted to ask but didn't think you should?

- Was your family very private in terms of feelings?

- To whom, if anyone, did you express your feelings?

- If you visited a sick relative in the hospital, or attended a funeral, were you prepared ahead of time?

- What scared or worried you?

- What helped? What was unhelpful or hurtful?

- Did your teachers and classmates know your situation? How did you feel about them knowing?

- Did you feel that you or your family were being judged (often a common response to such issues as divorce, suicide or violent death)?

- Did anyone belittle your grief, especially if it was the death of a pet?

- Were you given ample time and support to adjust to your new reality?

Knowing your own history and recognizing what was difficult for you will help you to better support your grieving students.

Identifying the grieving student

Before you can support your students, you need to know what is going on in their lives. Sometimes this will be obvious; at other times, you will have to read between the lines to recognize their inner turmoil. Clarifying with parents or guardians can be a useful way of keeping lines of communication open.

Here are some indicators that a child is grieving:

- a normally outgoing child becomes withdrawn;

- a well-adjusted child has temper outbursts or demonstrates aggressive behaviour;

- homework is uncharacteristically incomplete;

- the child is sleepy or appears listless and sad;

- the child has little appetite;

- the child cries easily;

- the child is unusually clingy.

Helping the grieving student

If you think you have identified a student who is grieving, here is some advice on how to handle the situation.

Confidentiality

Confidentiality is important in a trust relationship, but there are some things that teachers cannot keep secret. Before opening up a conversation, you must say to even your youngest students that if they tell you about something that is hurting them, that is putting them in danger or that is illegal, the law says you have to tell the principal and others who can help. Never promise to keep a secret without explaining this point first. Then ask if the student still wants to share with you. If the student says no, make sure he or she knows there is an open invitation to come back at any time, and that you will periodically check back with him or her.

Always respect the student's right not to share the loss with class-mates. When the situation does not require you to inform the principal, but you feel that the principal and other teachers could be of help, ask the student for permission to involve them. Explain that other adults at school can support the student, especially if you are away. Also, if the student happens to get into trouble, others may be more understanding if they know what is going on.

Explain that you will not tell parents or guardians what is shared, but be sure the student knows that you are in communication with home so that everyone can work together through this time of grieving. Usu-ally, students are glad that other adults want to help.

Initial *response to a disclosed loss*

- If you learn from a student, from the student's family, or from a friend or colleague that a loss has occurred, arrange to have some private time to talk with the student.

- If the news is second-hand, check with the student's family to make sure you haven't been misinformed.

- If you suspect that the family is in great turmoil (e.g., social services has become involved), let your principal know about your concern and your intention to talk to your student. It is always prudent to have backup support.

- If your school is near a women's shelter, you may have students in transition from time to time. Be welcoming, be sensitive and get some guidance from your principal or social workers (if your board has these services).

Approaching *a grieving student*

Whether a student tells you outright or you suspect that a student is grieving, you need to arrange some private time to talk. You might request special help at recess, or ask for assistance with an errand. Reassure the student that he or she is not in trouble and that this is a private time. (See the note on *Confidentiality* above.)

Students will usually tell their teachers if a pet has died, if they visited Grandpa in the hospital last night, or maybe even if an aunt "lost" a baby. Sometimes they blurt out the news to the whole class or reveal it during prayer time. Some students might find an opportunity to tell you as they linger before going out for recess. If students tell the whole class, be sure to express your care and concern and suggest a time to talk further. In private, you might ask for more information and begin the grief journey together.

Conversation starters

When meeting with the student, you may need to start the conversation. This gives the student permission to discuss feelings and be relieved of the burden of having to initiate the discussion. Here are some possible starters:

- "You told the class last week that your dog died. I was wondering if you would like to tell me about him."

- "You are going to your aunt's funeral tomorrow. Would you like to talk about what you think will happen?"

- "Your parents told me that you are moving to another city next month. You probably have lots of feelings about the move. Let's see if we can put names on those feelings."

- "Your brother has been in the hospital for a long time. Sometimes in class you seem very sad, and at other times you seem angry and fight with your friends. Would you like to talk about it?"

- "I know that your mom and dad have decided to separate. How are you feeling about that?"

Next Steps

Do not be discouraged if students do not want to express their feelings. Often it is enough for them to know they do not have to carry a burden alone, and that you are watching out for them. If you promise to chat again, make sure you are able to keep that promise. Some students will be very forthcoming about their feelings and circumstances over time; others may never really open up. That's fine – giving your time, care and attention does not require in-depth probing. For some suggested activities that will help you guide a student in future meetings, see Chapter 4.

Seeking professional support

If a student does not seem to respond, or is in great emotional distress, it is time to seek further help. Here are some signs that indicate a need for professional help:

- extreme, prolonged sadness;

- daydreaming;

- frequent crying;

- regression to earlier behaviours (e.g., thumb-sucking, loss of bladder or bowel control);

- violent actions;

- withdrawal from friends;

- physical self-mutilation; or

- talk of suicide.

Begin by talking with your principal about your concerns. Contact the parents or guardians. Explain your worries and ask if they see the same behaviour at home. Perhaps together you can discover ways to help the student. Begin by suggesting a visit to the family doctor, then offer names of agencies that work with bereaved children. Families may have access to a support group through their workplace benefits.

Some school boards or churches offer support programs, such as Rainbows: Restoring Hope to Grieving Youth.[1] If you don't have information about these local resources, ask the family to get referrals from their doctor. Further steps are beyond your mandate as an educator; teachers are not social workers or psychologists and there are boundaries beyond which you cannot go. Some families will be

---

[1] Rainbows provides support services and curricula for those suffering as a result of separation, divorce, death or other painful loss (www.rainbows.ca).

relieved that you have recognized a concern; others will be resistant to further suggestions.

Conclusion

Teachers play a significant role in walking with students through grief. Sometimes, teachers are the only constant in a shifting, scary world. Some students rely on teachers to care for them, let them feel their feelings appropriately, and provide a haven of routine amid changing circumstances.

Elementary teachers spend most of the day with their students. The teacher-student relationship goes far deeper than just delivering curriculum. Although you are not the only adult support as students journey through loss and grief, you are a big part of their lives. You enter their world to stand with them and become part of their journey. Frightened, lonely, sad, angry, grieving students cannot learn.

Elizabeth Kübler-Ross has said, "If the desperate child has one human being who cares, one person who can hear the often non-verbal plea for help, a disaster can often be prevented."[2] In the words of Pope John Paul II, "Do not be afraid!" As time goes by, your students will not remember the things you said, but they will be strengthened by the gift of your time, attention and knowledge.

In her book *Children in Crisis*, educator Fran Newman challenges each of us to be there for our hurting children with these words: "If not you, who? If not now, when?"[3] This is truly holy work!

---

[2] Cited in Fran Newman, *Children in Crisis* (Toronto: Scholastic, 1993), p. 204.
[3] Ibid., p. 205.

4

ONGOING SUPPORT FOR GRIEVING STUDENTS

This chapter contains strategies for walking through the grieving process with your student or class.

What to do

- Be certain that the information students receive is accurate. Incorrect information can often add to the confusion of loss.

- Share honest feelings about the loss. If the loss is a death, share your own memories of the person, such as "I will always remember Ricky's amazing sense of humour, even when he was so sick in hospital."

- Always be truthful, even in your efforts to protect the students from sadness. "Did it hurt when Sarah was in the car accident?" "Yes, it probably did hurt a lot. That is why she needs special care in the hospital now."

- Create a climate in which the students feel comfortable asking questions and know they will receive honest answers, even if the answer is "I don't know."

- Use correct terminology related to death. The person has died and is not just "gone away" or "asleep."

- Listen carefully so you can hear what students ask or say and not what you think they ought to ask or say.

- Bring a sensitive and caring attitude to the students' age-appropriate comments or grief responses.

- Allow students to express as many feelings as they are able or willing to share. Respect a range of responses, whether they involve quietness, questioning or emotional upset.

- Be sensitive to cultural differences in response to the loss. Help students become aware of culturally appropriate behaviour.

- Share your faith with the students to model an appropriate faith response. God loves us deeply and is with us in life and in death. God does not take someone to heaven because God needs another angel. God does not make natural catastrophes happen, and they are not a form of punishment. These occur as part of the unfolding way nature works.

- Recognize and expect the need of primary students to ask the same questions over and over.

- Involve the students as much as possible in tasks related to a remembrance or memorial ritual.

- Always respect a grieving student's wishes and share only the information he or she wants you to share with the class. When a family member is seriously ill or dying, some students may not want the whole class to know. You may want to spend time gently encouraging the student to give you permission to share this information so the class can offer support, be understanding and, as a community, pray for the person.

- Tell the student that you will share his or her loss with the principal and other staff persons who might be able to help.

- When the loss requires that the school stay in contact with the family, identify one school spokesperson so the family will not be overwhelmed with phone calls.

- Always ask for support when you feel you need it.

What not to do

- *Don't* say something in an artificial way in an effort to sound positive, such as "Don't worry, moms and dads fight all the time. Everything will be fine." *Do* bring a sense of hope in God to the discussion. "Even in times of trouble, God is always with us."

- *Don't* link loss, suffering or death with guilt, punishment or sin. *Don't* blame God by offering false comfort statements. God does not need the person in heaven and does not cause us to suffer because we did something wrong. *Do* help students to see how God is with them through the caring of other people.

- *Don't* try to correct students' feelings or comments unless they share inaccurate information. *Do* help them find ways to express feelings through movement, play or art.

- *Don't* lecture. A crisis is not the time to make a point or moralize about the event. *Do* take time to pray as a class, aloud or in silence.

- *Don't* force students to take part in a discussion. *Do* encourage them to find someone to talk to if they are struggling.

- *Don't* process a loss endlessly. Routines may need to be altered, but not discarded completely. You may need to return to the discussion from time to time. *Do* offer activities such as writing letters, cards or journals to give the students' grieving a sense of direction and focus.

- *Don't* say, "I know how you feel." *Do* say, "I can't imagine what this must be like for you, but I care about you very much and I am here for you."

- *Don't* tell students how they are to feel. *Do* give them space to discover how they feel and ways to express it.

- *Don't* overload students with information. *Do* give sufficient information and wait for their questions.

- *Don't* feel you have to fix the sadness and hurting. *Do* support the students' right to grieve.

- *Don't* readily dismiss or discount a student's loss because it may seem minor to you (i.e. a young child's loss of a favourite stuffed animal). *Do* help the student to cope with the loss and move forward.

- *Don't* take a whole class to the visitation at a funeral home. At the elementary level, that is the role of the parents. Even if the class attends a funeral Mass, parents need to be informed and be with their children.

Suggestions for specific situations

When the home environment is in crisis

In the event that a mother has "lost" her baby, discover what the student thinks this expression means and gently help him or her to understand if there is some confusion. It is important that the student knows that you are aware of the situation, you are watching out for him or her at school, and you are willing to talk.

In the event of a separation or divorce, parents may feel this is a private matter and not tell you. Some students will keep it to themselves that Daddy moved out last night. Others may tell everyone they meet about Mommy's new apartment.

You may need to take steps to approach the student. If you know that a separation is occurring, arrange a time to speak privately with the student. Say that you are aware that his or her parents are separating and that this might be a sad and confusing time. Students may be comfortable talking further or may just be glad that you know. Tell the student you will provide opportunities to talk again. Do not leave this entirely up to the student – take the initiative even if it feels as if your caring has been rejected.

The disruption of moving

When a student is moving away, affirm her or his sadness and fears about missing school and friends and give positive encouragement about the new adventure. Providing e-mail addresses could be a good way to show that you wish to stay connected. This might help the student feel less fearful and bereft.

When a new student arrives, a warm welcome is essential. Pair the student with a couple of trustworthy buddies until he or she finds new friends. Offer opportunities for new students to share about their background. Checking in with them privately can provide needed reassurance.

Be particularly vigilant with students who come as immigrants or refugees. Be a mentor for these newcomers, and invite other teachers and students to do the same. The more support they have, the smoother the transition will be.

If your school happens to be near a women's shelter, some of your students may be in your class for only a few weeks because of the transitory nature of their lives. Welcome them and make them feel at home as much as possible.

Situations involving the whole class

Sometimes situations occur that affect all of your students.

A Personal Story

Some years ago, I was asked to help a teacher tell his class about a Halloween prank that had gone terribly wrong. One of his students had accidentally shot another classmate in the eye with a pellet gun.

The teacher was magnificent in his caring, his tears and his non-judgmental approach toward both the one harmed and the one responsible for the harm. He calmed the class's fears, answered questions, allowed them their feelings and, when the time was right, gently led them back to some semblance of routine. Although he was very capable and had a great rapport with his students, he allowed them and me to see him when he was overwhelmed. He was a wise man in recognizing that there is strength, not shame, in being vulnerable. Teachers do not have to be rugged individualists!

Cathy Gross

Natural disasters such as flooding, tornado, fire or earthquake

In the past few years, we have experienced worldwide catastrophic events resulting in great loss. The following are examples of situations that can affect a whole class or school community and some suggestions for how to handle them.

When the disaster occurs in your region or involves your students' relatives, give students opportunities to tell their stories and give voice to their fears. Time for prayer, bulletin board displays, collages, scrapbooks, cards and letter-writing gives them something concrete to do so they do not feel helpless. With permission from the principal, a collection or small fund-raising project can give students a focus and a way to reach out and help.

When students see far-off disasters on television, they may be afraid that these can happen close to them. Teachers need to be appropriately reassuring. For example, instead of saying you will never have a flood even though you live near a major river, explain that emergency plans are in place and many people are specially trained to help and get people to safety ahead of time.

Serious illness, accident or death of a classmate, sibling, teacher or other staff member

Your principal generally will take the lead in these cases. Ideally, your board has a Crisis Response Plan in place to provide guidance. This can be a very emotional time. It is all right to cry with your students, but it is critical to have another adult to help you share the information with your class as soon as possible. In some boards, a religion consultant can support you as you reach out to your students.

School lock-down due to crime in the neighbourhood

Students may experience feelings of terror when the school is locked down because of criminal activity in the area (a serious crime has been committed in the neighbourhood, or vandalism has been done to your school). Rely on your principal or a designated person to be the spokesperson for the school who will convey accurate information to the staff.

Try to prevent rumours from starting. Give your students the opportunity to put names on their feelings and to take control of their fears. If possible, when the time is right, invite a police officer to speak to the class. Reassure the students that they are safe.

Re-establishing routines

In all the above cases, it is important for students to return to normal routines after a reasonable time has been taken for discussion and related activities. Provide more individual support for students who are most affected. Deal with the loss again as a class at a later time as long as there is a need. It can be helpful and meaningful to mark the one-month, six-month and first-year anniversaries with a special prayer or prayer service so the students know that the loss is not forgotten.

Helpful strategies

As teachers, we can play an important role in helping students express their wants, needs and feelings with words rather than by acting out in negative or hurtful ways.

- Provide opportunities for music, poetry, journalling and art.

- Ask students to complete sentences such as

– I feel like crying when…

– I feel sad when…

– I feel worried when…

– I am frightened that…

Assure them that all these feelings are normal. Everyone who has had a loss experiences some or all of these feelings.

- Invite young children to draw a picture of their heart or the weather inside of them to express their feelings and anxieties.[4]

- Offer young children creative play with puppets or action figures, as it is easier for them to express feelings by projecting them onto inanimate objects.

- Read a story about loss with the student and invite him or her to share the book at home.

- Create a memory book or journal to show that a deceased person's life or the life of a friend living far away has value.

[4] Ann Murphy, *Living with Death* (York Catholic District School Board, 1995).

Conclusion

This book highlights the importance and the need for prayer in dealing with the losses of our lives. Faith and hope in God's great love for us provide the foundation for meaningful prayer. When the loss is a death, ceremonies of remembrance bring healing.

In our prayer, we ask for God's guidance that we may grow in strength, hope and trust. When we are grieving, the future often feels and looks uncertain. Grieving is a long process; we need to be patient. There are no quick and easy solutions. As the Book of Ecclesiastes reminds us:

> *For everything there is a season,*
> *and a time for every matter under heaven:*
> *a time to be born, and a time to die…*
> *a time to weep, and a time to laugh;*
> *a time to mourn, and a time to dance… (3.1 ff.)*

New life that can emerge from life's losses will express both continuity and transformation. The caterpillar becomes a beautiful butterfly. The seed becomes a plant or flower. The egg becomes a chick. When Jesus rose from the dead, he was the same Jesus, but he was different. Even some of his disciples did not recognize him in his new life.

As your students move through the grieving process, they too will undergo great changes. With the grace of God and the help of caring teachers, they will emerge stronger in their understanding of life's sorrows and with increased empathy for all who experience loss.

Prayers for Times of Loss

This section contains prayers designed for elementary students as well as a liturgy for the school or class at the elementary level.

When a student or staff member dies, it is customary for the teacher to tell the students and then to pray a brief prayer with them. A crisis team may be in the school to help staff and students cope with the loss. A Mass may be celebrated or a liturgy held later in the week.

Reflection – God is with us in our sadness

(Kindergarten to Grade 4)

Ask the children to sit quietly and listen with their ears and with their hearts. If you wish, dim the lights and play instrumental music. Invite the children to close their eyes.

> Think of a time when you felt sad because you had lost something you really loved. It might have been a favourite toy, a close friend who moved away, a pet that died. Maybe you were lost, or your family was moving to a new home.
>
> If you can remember one time like that, then try to remember what made it better. Did somebody say, "Don't worry, I'll be there to help you"? Did somebody give you a hug?
>
> Now that you're bigger, would you still be unhappy if the same thing happened to you? Or are there different things that make you feel sad and alone now? What would help to make it better?
>
> Everybody feels sad sometimes. Everybody feels afraid or helpless sometimes.
>
> God is like the person who hugs you and says, "I'll be there with you." God is with us all the time, whether we are happy or sad. No matter what happens to you, you can be sure that God loves you.
>
> The love of God can make you feel better even at the worst of times.
>
> Take a few moments to talk to God in your heart. Tell God if you are sad about something, and remember that God is always with you.

Play or sing an appropriate hymn.

Reflection – When Something Truly Sad Has Happened
(Grades 5 and up)

Use this prayer in a time of crisis, such as a death or serious illness, or in the face of terrible news events or natural disasters that students are concerned about.

Invite students to sit comfortably and quietly as you offer this prayer of reflection.

Sometimes we feel so sad that we don't know how to pray.

At times like those, it helps to remember that the Spirit of God
　　lives within us.
God knows us even better than we know ourselves.
God knows how we feel, even when we can't say our feelings
　　in words.
The Spirit of God will help us in our sadness.

No matter what happens, God wants to help us.
God gives us the strength to keep going.
God's love is stronger than sorrow and death.
God's love is forever.

I am sure that nothing can separate us from the love of God:
not hunger, not danger, not any other creature in the world, not life,
　　and not death.
Nothing can separate us from the love of God.

(Adapted from Romans 8:26-27, 38)

Play or sing an appropriate hymn.

Prayer in time of loss and suffering

(all levels – can be simplified for younger students)

Leader:

> A good friend is always faithful.
> God is our friend.
> God is always faithful.
> We can trust that God will remain with us in our sadness.

Read Mark 4:35-41, below (Jesus calms the storm).
Tell students that Jesus has just spent the day healing the sick and telling thousands of people about God and God's great love for them. He is very tired and needs to rest.

On that day, when evening had come, he said to them, "Let us go across to the other side." And leaving the crowd behind, they took him with them in the boat, just as he was. Other boats were with him. A great windstorm arose, and the waves beat into the boat, so that the boat was already being swamped. But he was in the stern, asleep on the cushion; and they woke him up and said to him, "Teacher, do you not care that we are perishing?" He woke up and rebuked the wind, and said to the sea, "Peace! Be still!" Then the wind ceased, and there was a dead calm. He said to them, "Why are you afraid? Have you still no faith?" And they were filled with great awe and said to one another, "Who then is this, that even the wind and the sea obey him?" (Mark 4:35-41)

Reflection

All of us have storms in our lives. When we lose someone or something we really love, we may feel as if we are all alone, and that no one cares. But Jesus always cares. When the storm is too much for us, when our sorrows are too heavy for us to bear, he is there to calm the storm. Think about the storms in your life. Who was there to calm your fears? Who comforted you? Through the love of these people, Jesus came to you and offered to calm the waters. All he asks is that you have faith: that you continue to hope and know that he is present in those who love and support you.

Concluding prayer

Faithful God, this is a difficult time for us. We need your help and the help of others. Give us the strength and courage to believe there is hope. We know you are with us in this time of worry and fear. Help us to recognize your presence. **Amen**.

Prayer – When someone we love dies

(Grades 5 and up)

Loving Jesus,
Through your life, death and resurrection you taught us that God
　　never abandons us.
You promised that we would share in God's gift of eternal life and
　　happiness.
We believe.
Open your loving arms to receive _____,
who has died and awaits your welcome.

We know you are with us in our sorrow.
Help us to accept the pain that accompanies the loss of someone
　　we love.
Help us to understand that we must die in order to live with you
　　forever.
Like a seed that falls to the ground, we must die to our earthly
　　bodies to be reborn with you.
Help us to accept this mystery of life in faith, for it is beyond our
　　understanding.

Jesus, we trust that you are with us in our sorrow.
We thank you for your steadfast love.
We praise you, for you have overcome sadness and death forever.
Amen.

Psalm 27 (adapted)
(Grades 3 to 6)

Response: God is my light and my strength.

God is my light, helping me to see hope in my sorrow;
I shall not be afraid.
God is my source of strength;
I shall face my losses with courage.   R.

O God, hear my voice when I call out to you;
please have mercy on me and answer my prayers.
It is your face, O God, that I seek;
do not hide your face from me.   R.

I am sure I shall see the Lord's goodness
in the land of the living.
Hope in God, be strong and have courage:
Hope in God!   R.

A blessing for those who grieve
(Grade 3 and up)

May God hear you as you cry out in sorrow;
May God wipe away all your tears;
May you know God's love through those who comfort you;
May you feel God's arms around you in the hugs you receive from
    your friends and family;
May you hear God's voice in the prayers people pray for you;
And may God's joy fill your heart
    when others give you a reason to smile.

Prayer service for students when a death occurs
(All grades)

This service can be used as a school liturgy or can help you prepare for the celebration of a memorial Mass.

Introduction

Jesus told us that where two or more are gathered in his name, he is there with us. We trust that as we gather here today to pray for our friend/classmate _____, Jesus is with us. Let us be still for a moment and welcome Jesus into our midst. (*brief pause while students settle and become silent*)

Through his life, death and resurrection, Jesus shows us how to pray in times of sorrow and how to accept the sorrows of this life. He prayed for the courage to overcome his fear, and prayed to God in all times of need. He taught us to pray, too.

By his example, Christ is our light that overcomes the darkness of our sorrow. When we place our trust in him, he will take away our fear and guide us through the pain of our losses. He is our comfort and our strength. The light of Christ is our hope and our promise of new life.

Invite the assembly to stand and join in singing the hymn.

Hymn: (*can be sung while lighting a candle*) "*Children of the Light*" (Come and See *catechetical program [Canadian Conference of Catholic Bishops]. Year 4, #12) or another appropriate hymn*

First Reading (Joshua 1:9)
A reading from the book of Joshua.

Be strong and courageous;
do not be frightened or dismayed,
for the Lord your God is with you wherever you go.
The word of the Lord.
Thanks be to God.

Responsorial Psalm (Psalm 84; adapted for children)
Response: O God, we thank you for your endless love.

How lovely is your home, O God.
My whole being wants to be with you.
My heart and lips sing for joy to you, O living God.   R.

Even the sparrow finds a home,
and the swallow, a nest for herself,
where she can lay her young before you.
Happy are those who live with you.
They will always sing your praise.   R.

Happy are the people who have you for a friend;
happy are they who feel strong because they trust in your ways.
You wipe away all sadness and fill their lives with joy.
They are strong and have no fear.   R.

Hear our prayer, O God.
Look upon the face of your friends.
I would rather spend one day with you
than a thousand with those who choose to do wrong.
Lord, you give light to our eyes and protect us from harm.
Blessed are those who hope and trust in you.   R.

Gospel Acclamation (sung) John 11:25-26

Alleluia (outside of Lent)

Praise to you, Lord, king of eternal glory (during Lent)

I am the resurrection and the life, says the Lord.
Those who believe in me will never die.

Gospel (John 14:1-3)

A reading from the holy gospel according to John.

Glory to you, Lord.

Jesus said to his disciples:
"Do not let your hearts be troubled.
Believe in God, believe also in me.
In my Father's house there are many dwelling places.
If it were not so, would I have told you that I go to prepare a place
    for you?
And if I go and prepare a place for you,
I will come again and will take you to myself,
so that where I am, there you may be also."

The gospel of the Lord.

Praise to you, Lord Jesus Christ.

General Intercessions

The response to each petition is: **O God, we know you are with us.**

For our friend _____, and for all those who
    care for him/her, we pray…   R.

For all people who are suffering loss and seeking hope and comfort
    in your promise of resurrection and new life, we pray…   R.

51

For those who have no hope, we pray… R.

For the sad and the lonely, including ourselves, we pray… R.

For all the quiet yearnings of our hearts, we pray… R.

Presentation

If students have created cards or memory boxes in honour of the deceased, these could be brought up at this point and either laid on a prayer table or altar or given to a representative of the family.

Leader: Let us pray.

God has chosen you to be his hands in this world. Go now and be Christ to one another, be comfort for those who mourn, be hope to those in despair, be joy to those who weep. Go in peace in the name of the Father, and of the Son, and of the Holy Spirit.

Amen.

Closing hymn: "We Are Many Parts," "Taste and See" (In the Spirit We Belong catechetical program [Canadian Conference of Catholic Bishops]. Year 3, #8) *or another appropriate hymn.*

Resources

The following is a brief list of helpful books (organized by theme) to help you support children living with loss. Primary books are also excellent tools for facilitating discussion with older children.

Books for children

Death

Burrowes, Adjoa. *Grandma's Purple Flowers*. New York: Lee and Low Books, 2000. (A young girl recalls visits with her grandmother during each season of the year, until the winter that her grandmother dies.)

Buscaglia, Leo. *The Fall of Freddie the Leaf: A Story of Life for All Ages*. Toronto: Holt Rinehart and Winston, 1982. (As Freddie experiences the changing seasons along with the other leaves, he learns about the cycle of life/death/new life.)

Clifton, Lucille. *Everett Anderson's Good-bye*. New York: Henry Holt and Company, 1983. (Everett Anderson has a hard time coming to terms with his grief after his father dies.)

Cohen, Janet, D.S.W. *I Had a Friend Named Peter*. New York: Morrow, 1987. (When Betsy's friend dies, Betsy's parents and teacher answer her questions about dying, funerals and the burial process.)

dePaola, Tomie. *Nana Upstairs & Nana Downstairs*. New York: Penguin, 2000. (Tommy, who has a good relationship with both his grandmother and great-grandmother, must eventually learn to accept their deaths.)

Goble, Paul. *Beyond the Ridge*. New York: Bradbury Press, 1989. (A spiritual journey into the afterlife – beyond the ridge – as experienced through the death of a Plains Indian grandmother and her grieving loved ones.)

Grossnickle Hines, Ann. *Remember the Butterflies*. New York: Dutton Press, 1991. (When their grandpa dies, Holly and Glen remember the special times they had with him, gardening, reading and learning about butterflies.)

McFarlane, Sheryl. *Waiting for the Whales*. Victoria: Orca, 1991. (A lonely old man who waits each year to see the orcas swim past his house imparts his love of the whales to his granddaughter. This book suggests that aging and death are part of a larger cycle of rebirth and continuity.)

McLaughlin, Kirsten. *The Memory Box*. Omaha, NE: Centering Corporation, 2001. (A young boy, mourning the loss of his grandfather, fills a memory box with things that remind him of times they spent together.)

Munsch, Robert. *Love You Forever*. Toronto: Firefly Books, 1986.

Quinlan, Patricia. *Tiger Flowers*. Toronto: Lester Publishing, 1994. (A beloved uncle dies of AIDS.)

Sanford, Doris. *It Must Hurt a Lot: A Book about Death, and Learning, and Growing*. Portland, OR: Multnomah Press, 1986. (Describes a boy's reactions of anger, grief and eventual acceptance when his dog dies. Includes suggestions for helping a child deal with loss.)

Tiffault, B.W. *A Quilt for Elizabeth*. Omaha, NE: Centering Corporation, 1992. (Elizabeth displays anger over her father's illness and denial when he dies. Gradually, with the help of her mother and grandmother, she comes to accept his absence.)

Wood, Douglas. *Grandad's Prayers of the Earth*. Boston: Candlewick Publications, 2002. (Grandad explains how all things in the natural world pray and make a gift to the beauty of life, so when he dies his grandson finds comfort.)

Yeomans, E. *Lost and Found: Remembering a Sister*. Omaha, NE: Centering Corporation, 2000. (A preschool girl recounts her confusing thoughts and feelings after the death of her sister and the number of ways she continues to feel her sister's love.)

Divorce

Goff, Beth Twiggar. *Where Is Daddy? The Story of Divorce*. Boston: Beacon Press, 1985. (A book on divorce for young children.)

Menendez-Aponte, Emily. *When Mom and Dad Divorce: A Kid's Resource*. Abbey Press, Elf-help Books for Kids, 2000. (A book about divorce for children ages 5 to 8.)

Stinson, Kathy. *Mom and Dad Don't Live Together Any More*. Toronto: Annick Press, 1984.

God's love for us

Wise Brown, Margaret. *The Runaway Bunny*. New York: HarperCollins Publishers, 1972. (A profoundly comforting story of a bunny's imaginary game of hide-and-seek and the lovingly steadfast mother who finds him every time. A profound metaphor for God as mother.)

Moving

McKend, Heather. *Moving Gives Me a Stomach Ache*. North York, ON: Discis Knowledge Research, 1990. (A story about moving and a child's emotions during this upheaval.)

Muller, Robin. *Badger's New House*. Toronto: North Winds Press, 2002. (After moving into a new house and fixing up his old one for his grandmother, Badger realizes that he misses his former home.)

Books for Adults

Cooper, Noel. *Language of the Heart: How to Read the Bible* (A User's Guide for Catholics). Ottawa: Novalis, 2003. (An award-winning, user-friendly introduction to the Bible. Offers language and explanations that help with understanding the concept of God-with-us in our losses rather than the cause of these losses.)

Fitzgerald, Helen. *The Grieving Child*. New York: Simon and Schuster, 1992. (Provides guidance for explaining death to a child, covering such areas as visiting the seriously ill or dying, difficult situations such as suicide and murder, attending a funeral, and the role of faith.)

Grollman, Rabbi Earl. *Bereaved Children and Teens: A Support Guide for Parents and Professionals*. Boston: Beacon Press, 1996. (A comprehensive guide to helping children and teens cope with the emotional, religious, social and physical effects of a loved one's death.)

Kroen, William C. *Helping Children Cope with the Loss of a Loved One: A Guide for Grownups*. Minneapolis, MN: Free Spirit Publishing. (Sound advice, comfort and compassion for adults who are helping a child cope with death.)

Wezeman, Phyllis, Jude Dennis Fournier and Kenneth Wezeman. *Guiding Children Through Life's Losses: Prayer, Rituals and Activities*. Mystic, CT: Twenty-Third Publications, 1998. (Prayers and activities to guide and support children coping with ordinary and extraordinary life losses. Encourages children to look through the lens of faith and hope as they deal with their loss.)